Simone Fattal
A breeze over the Mediterranean

Fondazione ICA Milano
Pompeii Commitment. Archaeological Matters

Alberto Salvadori, Andrea Viliani

Memento Vitae…
A Breeze, Once Again, and Together

A breeze over the Mediterranean is the title of Simone Fattal's first solo exhibition in Italy, curated by Alberto Salvadori with Andrea Viliani, Stella Bottai, and Laura Mariano. Its breeze wafted from the headquarters of Fondazione ICA Milano for a few months—from September 8, 2021, to January 9, 2022—bringing with it inspirations drawn from the artist's research conducted at the Archaeological Park of Pompeii within the context of the *Pompeii Commitment. Archaeological Matters* program. The exhibition was a chapter of the *Ceramics* program devised by Fondazione ICA Milano to explore ceramic as an artistic medium via works spanning from the twentieth century to the present day. Furthermore, on the occasion of the exhibition, the Archaeological Park of Pompeii inaugurated its own contemporary art collection, *Collectio*, acquiring as its first piece Fattal's ceramic sculpture *Hermes* (2021), named for the messenger of the gods who, at least in Pompeii, seems to have either neglected his work or gone unheard. But was this really the case?

Fattal was born in Syria and raised in Lebanon, where she studied philosophy at the École des Lettres in Beirut. After continuing her philosophical studies at the Université de la Sorbonne in Paris and initiating her artistic research in 1969 back in Beirut, she left in 1980, five years into the country's civil war, and moved to California. There she founded Post-Apollo Press, a publishing house specializing in experimental literary works. In 1988 she enrolled at the Art Institute of San Francisco, where she experimented for the first time with ceramics, which would become a recurring material in her sculptural practice even after her move to Paris in 2017, where she still lives and works.

Over the last fifty years, Fattal has consistently explored the episteme of archaeology and mythology, drawing from a range of sources, including ancient history, modern poetry, war narratives, and landscape painting, merging history with memory, addressing losses caused by the passage of time, and revealing recurrences and repetitions. Fattal's research has developed throughout her life as an independent artist, with many roots and many uprootings, articulated through the use of different expressive means, from sculpture and ceramics to drawing and painting. Fattal brings forth from the material, such as the natural and living clay, both abstract and figurative forms, evoking the union between carnal experience and mystical vision, between the reality of history and the surreality of the archetype. She shapes metamorphic figures that express the deepest intimacy of our thoughts, feelings, and dreams, grounding them in the experience of her life. The works give the lives of humans and every other creature the value of something fragile and fleeting, yet tenacious and irreducible.

Fattal resembles Pompeii in this sense, just as Pompeii resembles Fattal.

At the beginning of 2020, at the invitation of *Pompeii Commitment. Archaeological Matters*, the artist visited the city's Archaeological Park to study the site and its deposits in person, conducting research that would culminate in the reflections and sculptural representations of *A breeze over the Mediterranean* at Fondazione ICA Milano. To approach and reshape the Pompeian archetype in her own way, Fattal initially created a series of six collages on cardboard accompanied by notes, written in the manner of a personal diary, which were published on January 21, 2021, on the platform of the digital research center pompeiicommitment.org. In these collages, she juxtaposed visual fragments belonging to different geographies, historical periods, belief systems, and iconographies. Examples include the mosaic of the House of Orion—a depiction of one of the darkest myths of the ancient world, probably originating from Pharaonic Egypt—and the Memento Mori mosaic, symbolizing the mutable nature of fate and the inevitability of death. These Pompeian references were accompanied by cutouts (additional fragments) of images from other archaeological sites, for instance statues and artifacts from ancient Mediterranean civilizations, from Greece to Africa, paintings from the history of modern European art, such as *The Four Philosophers* by Peter Paul Rubens (1611–12), ancestral expressive forms, like the hand paintings by prehistoric artists in Argentina's Cueva de las Manos (ca. 7300 BCE), up to images of contemporary objects. In these collages, Fattal, who in her work prefers fragmented and compendious traits, began to observe universal history and the multiple individual stories of Pompeii as a continuous movement and a temporal short circuit, a tangled mixture of animal, mineral, and vegetable elements, of religious and social functions, of spurious iconographies that are continually quoted and quotable. These heterogeneous ensembles, despite their multi-species nature and residual consistency, are condensed in the spatio-temporal *punctum* of the individual fragments with which they have come down to us. *Pompeii, Today* is the title of the artist's final contribution to *Pompeii Commitment. Archaeological Matters*.

"Unlike all the other archaeological sites," says Fattal, "Pompeii already offers a reconstruction of itself, for the place was destroyed not by time, but by a moment. . . . Generally ruins in the world can be read on many levels, but there are fragments of all periods mingled together, or on top of each other. We need to reconstruct—level by level, fragment by fragment—their origins, relationships and influences, the sequence in time. In Pompeii, it's a fixed image." And it is precisely the "fixed" image of Pompeii's ruins that allows for the coexistence of intense and reciprocal influences of a time extended but concentrated in a single moment, as well as a space surrounding but expanded to all its relationships. In the artist's words, Pompeii is also "Egypt . . . but also Syria, Lebanon, Asia Minor, North Africa." Fattal evokes not a city in ruins, but an amalgam, a jumble, a mixture, a compost, where all distinctions between life and death, history (*historia*) and myth (*fabula*), nature and culture, human and nonhuman, are canceled. Its multiple meanings and possible interpretations correspond to a material through which the same breeze flows over the different Mediterranean cultures, blending them with one another and with the ecosystem that hosts them, where they are still available to our gaze. In observing them, we co-participate in their incessant transformation in which the fatal instant of their destruction is preserved, which they continue to embody: *memento mori* as much as *memento vitae*.

Such a mixture of contradictions and potentials, of past and present, was harmoniously regenerated in the sculptures molded, fired, colored, and glazed by the artist in 2021 at the renowned Bottega Gatti in Faenza—famous also for their secret recipes for iridescent glazes—and exhibited at Fondazione ICA Milano. As many as thirty-four works generated as part of the project and produced for the exhibition inhabited the rooms on the first floor, creating a gateway into history by evoking mythological characters, architectures, and natural elements. The choral ensemble of narrations, ancestral subjects, and archetypal forms defined a spatiotemporal otherness, taking itself and everyone on a journey with Fattal.

Despite its small size, the work *Ra with Isis* (2021) was one of the most emblematic in the exhibition. The figure of Ra gathers around itself the primitive syncretic speculation embodying the funeral as a transmission of powers and values, with Maat, the "Truth," being one of his daughters. Displayed in the center of an otherwise empty room was this small sculpture depicting Isis assisting her father in his final moments of life as he confers his magical powers on her, making her one of the most important deities of mourning, healing, and motherhood. In the sculpture *Europa and the Sacred Bull* (2021), Fattal represents the titular Phoenician princess embracing the bull—Zeus in one of his animal disguises—who transports her from her native Sidon, now Lebanon, to Crete. Europa's arms gently wrap around the bull's neck in an eternal image of love and exile. *Anubis* (2021)—named for the Egyptian god protector of the dead—rose as the most imposing sculpture in the exhibition. Positioned in the large central hall, his figure was slightly set apart and towered mysteriously over the other sculptures, evoking the cultural fusion and richness generated in the history—fluctuating among its countless histories—of the Mediterranean.

These works became companions on a journey between life and death, between the ghostliness of bodies and actions that once were and the physical concreteness of their memory, between their belonging to an imaginary universe and their appearance in our universe. Repeating, once again and for the last time, the artist's words: "My sculpture tries to recapture the living element of the moment that brought death. My sculpture wants these moments to live eternally, being close to the place and that day, and give them back to life."

The book you are about to read is the story of how all this became possible. Once again, and together with you, Simone Fattal.

Simone Fattal

A breeze over the Mediterranean

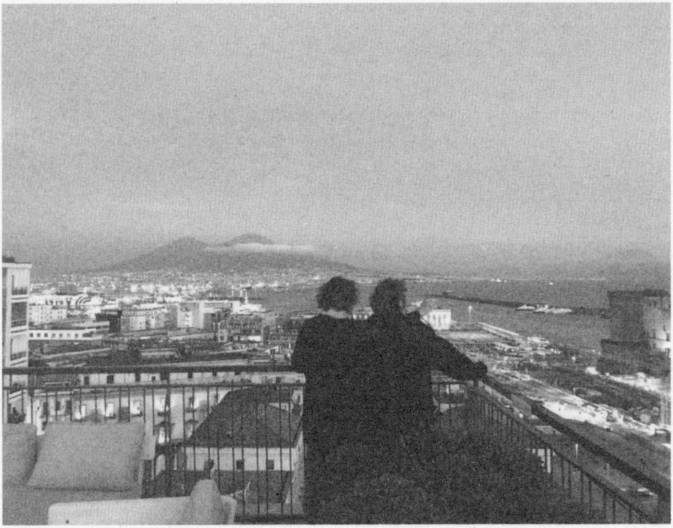

Simone Fattal, trip to Naples and Pompeii, February 2020

I arrived at the airport of Naples at the invitation of the Fondazione ICA Milano and *Pompeii Commitment. Archeological Matters*, for a visit of Pompeii.

20

The first thing I saw at the airport was a statue of Hermes, all red, in the face and all over.

My reaction was: Oh, he did not arrive in time to warn the citizens of Pompeii and Herculaneum of the impending disaster.

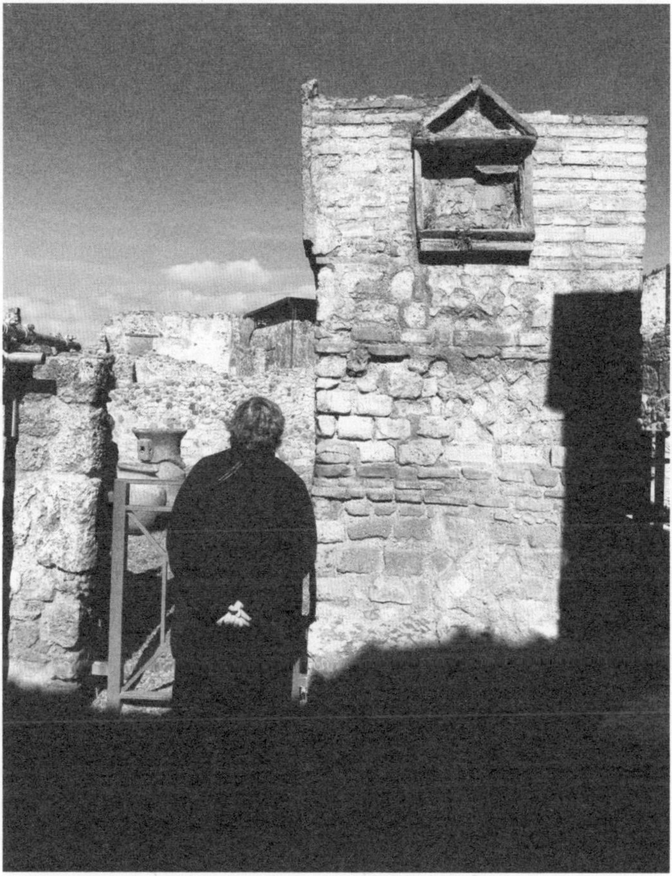

Simone Fattal, trip to Naples and Pompeii, February 2020

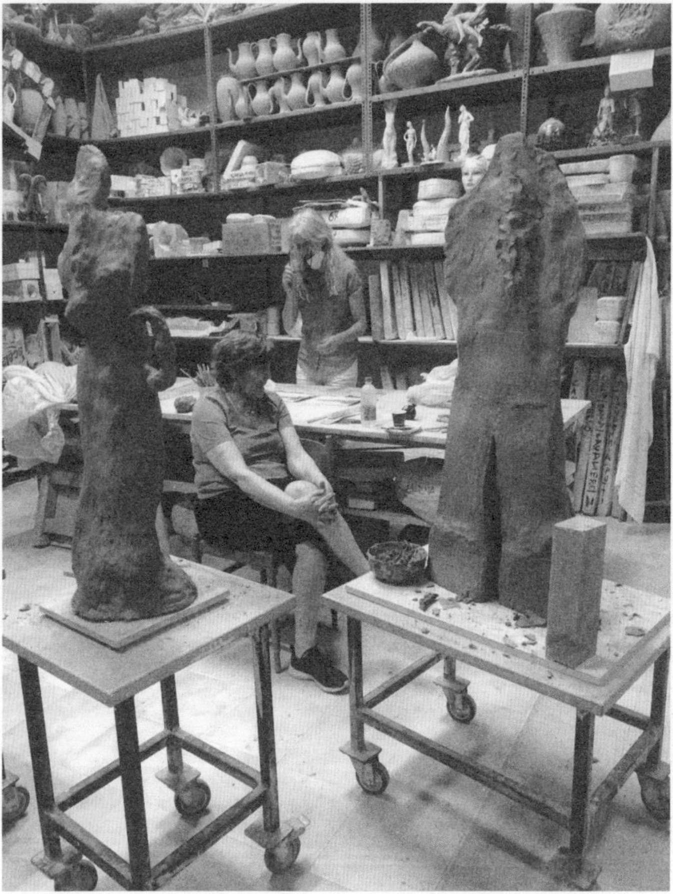

Simone Fattal at work, Ceramica Gatti, Faenza, February 2020

This image was the first I set out to do as soon as I arrived at the wonderful Bottega Gatti to prepare for my exhibition.

Hermes.
Hermes travels the airs; he embodies the link between all the Mediterranean shores. From the time the Egyptians came to Greece, and the Phoenicians to all the Mediterranean shores.

Shores which will ease into the Roman Empire.

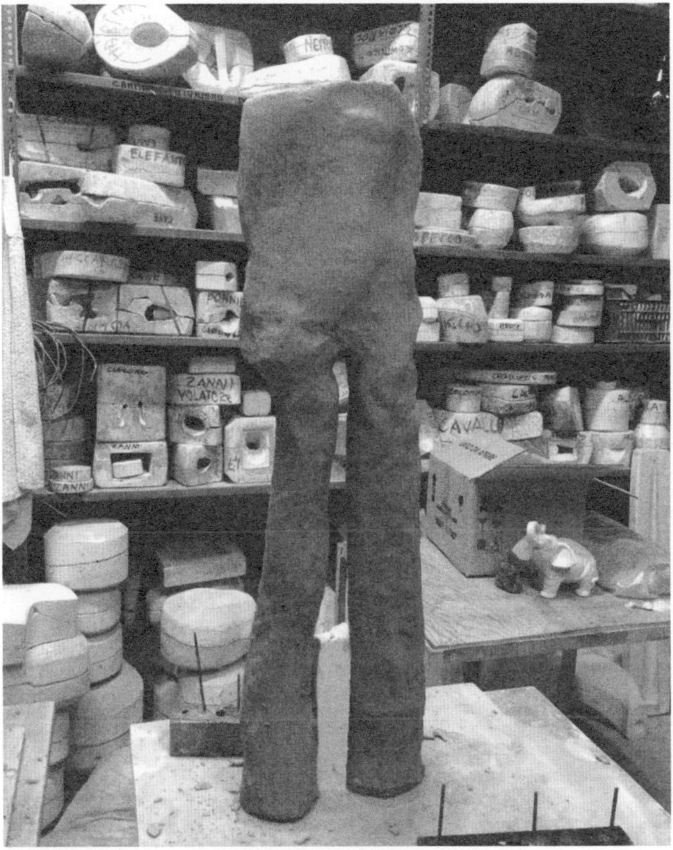

Simone Fattal, works in production, Ceramica Gatti, Faenza, February 2020

26

I found in Pompeii, as I had in Delos, the Temple of Isis.

Isis, I saw standing by the bed of her father, Ra, extorting from him THE GREAT NAME, which was the core of his strength, and which, as he was ill, he gave away.

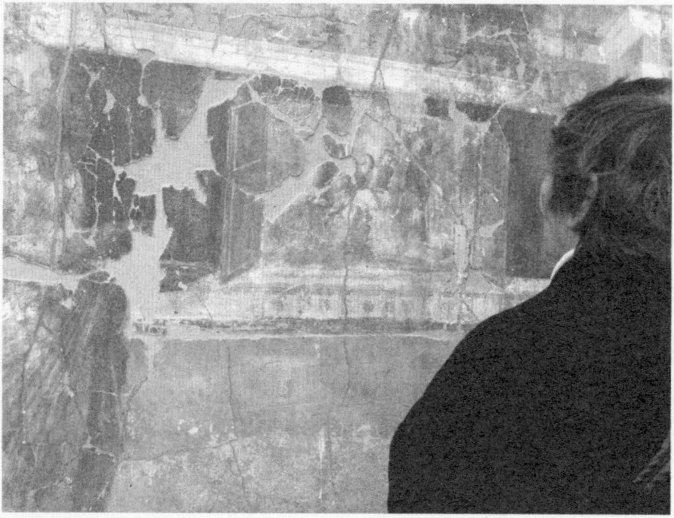

Simone Fattal, trip to Naples and Pompeii, February 2020

I saw Europe fleeing her native Sidon on the shoulders of the divine bull.

And most of all I started to apprehend a little the meaning of the Mysteries.

A young woman is taken to her initiation by an elder.

The young men are all around, also participating in the game of life and death.

Death is there, omnipresent, taking you to the eternal life.

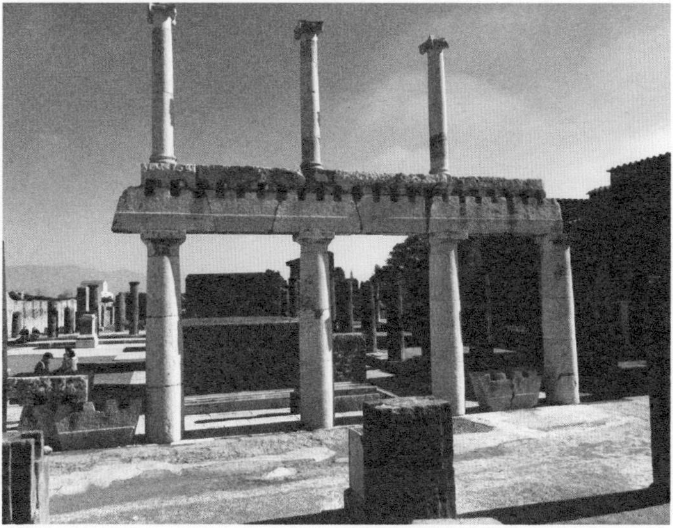

Simone Fattal, trip to Naples and Pompeii, February 2020

Etel Adnan

Simone Fattal, Ceramic Sculptor

Looking one day at the way Simone Fattal was holding in her hands eggplants that she had just bought, I felt that she had a special rapport with these objects—to which one pays no attention—and I thought that such a suitability between her hands and these eggplants could certainly suggest that she had an attraction to, an affinity with, forms and therefore with sculpture.

She was then a painter, living in Lebanon. But a few years later, the civil war in Lebanon led her to leave for California. She departed her Beirut studio with great sorrow. Once settled in the outskirts of San Francisco, she heard about a college with a good sculpture department. She enrolled. We should remember here that the American way of teaching is particularly open. The teacher stimulates, more than dictates or imposes a particular style or method. Thus, at the beginning of course, the teacher asked the students to choose a piece among many

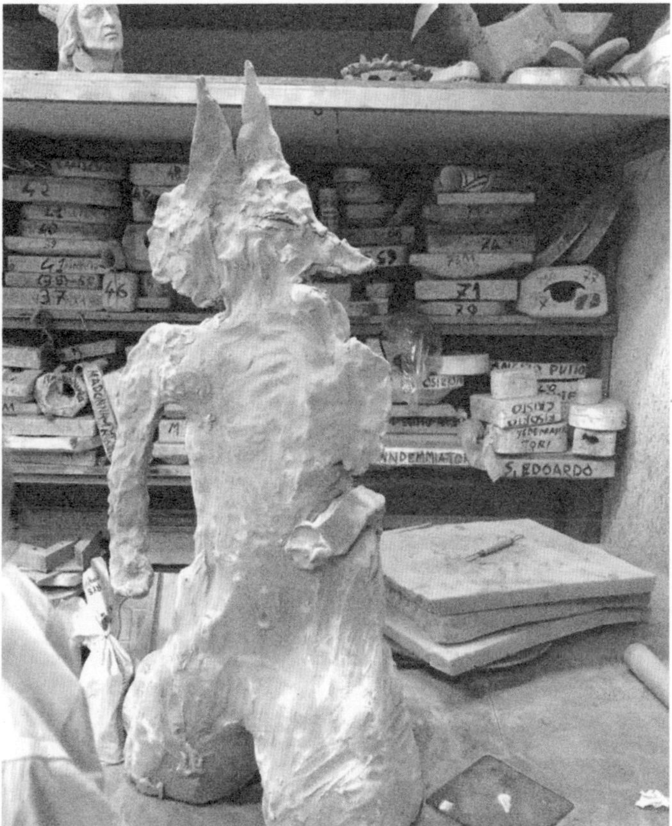

Simone Fattal, works in production, Ceramica Gatti, Faenza, February 2020

different materials. Fattal chose a big alabaster stone, although he insisted on a smaller one for a first try. She liked this translucent rock very much. In a quick glance, she assessed the stone's possibilities. She worked on it without forcing it, and the result was surprisingly right and beautiful. The pink alabaster, luminous, almost sensual, had become a statue bust one might have found at an archaeological site, only this time the archaeology was of a contemporary site. It was as if the war, which was still ravaging Lebanon thousands of miles away, were fusing with this unique piece. It was an enchantment for the eye and the mind. Besides, the artist has said herself that when looking at the stone, she made that link.

The following year, Fattal enrolled at the San Francisco Art Institute. This institute was one of the three or four more prestigious art schools in the United States. Celebrities such as Jackson Pollock, Ansel Adams, Diego Rivera,

Richard Diebenkorn, and others taught there during the golden years when American art dominated the art world. Fattal realized immediately that among all the disciplines taught at the Art Institute, ceramics appealed to her the most. Clay is probably the first material that humans privileged for their creations. It is not surprising that many ancient cultures believed that humans had been made by a god, or by God, from clay. Clay is pure earth, albeit particular, varied, and unique, soft and resistant, fragile and yet able to survive centuries, as good for the making of objects for everyday use as for conceptual artworks. Ceramics is the domain of infinite knowledge. In countries like Japan, China, and Korea, ceramics reach prices that are given in the West only to great paintings. Now even in the West things are changing, and ceramic pieces are more and more appreciated, approaching equal footing with works in bronze, iron, or steel.

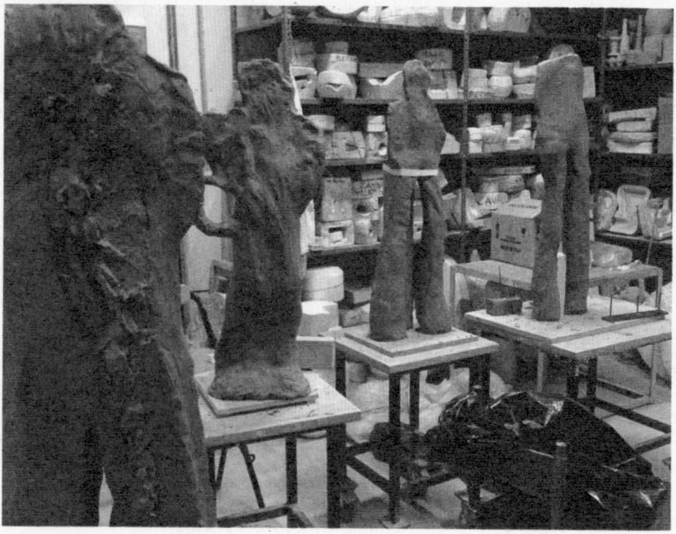

Simone Fattal, works in production, Ceramica Gatti, Faenza, February 2020

For amateurs, ceramics touch the sensibility because of the variety of colors which are natural to clay, and that no painting can equal. Moreover, the more one thinks about it, the more this material, once fired, represents an extraordinary dilemma. It's an art of fire and malleability that transforms these two elements into objects that are cold, fixed in their form for an infinite time.

When Fattal faced her first chunk of clay, she did not hesitate. Her fingers—that is, the deepest forces of her mind—made out of this muddy mass a person standing. It was an act of creation. She found her world immediately. She re-created in one stroke the first man of prehistoric times, and she created him standing. She created not an object, but a surge, a movement, an essential movement, the one that separates the human species from the animal world, which is, at the same time, akin to him.

She continued and still continues to make standing figures. They come as if naturally out of her hands. It is as if they are asking to be born out of the clay. It is as if they have always been there, and their creation is their liberation. They have the breath of life. They project not rigidity, but firmness. They are not anonymous. They are men or women, heroes of the past or mythic characters. We don't see them; we recognize them. They stand at the threshold of what makes the essence of their being. They are neither abstract nor realistic, but come from very far away, carrying in them the matter with which they were born. They haunt us, because we recognize them although we have never seen them before.

They have also this inexplicable power to be present while remaining mysterious; held in their silence, linked to instantaneity and still belonging to an unlimited (undefined?) time. In the philosophy of today, where a

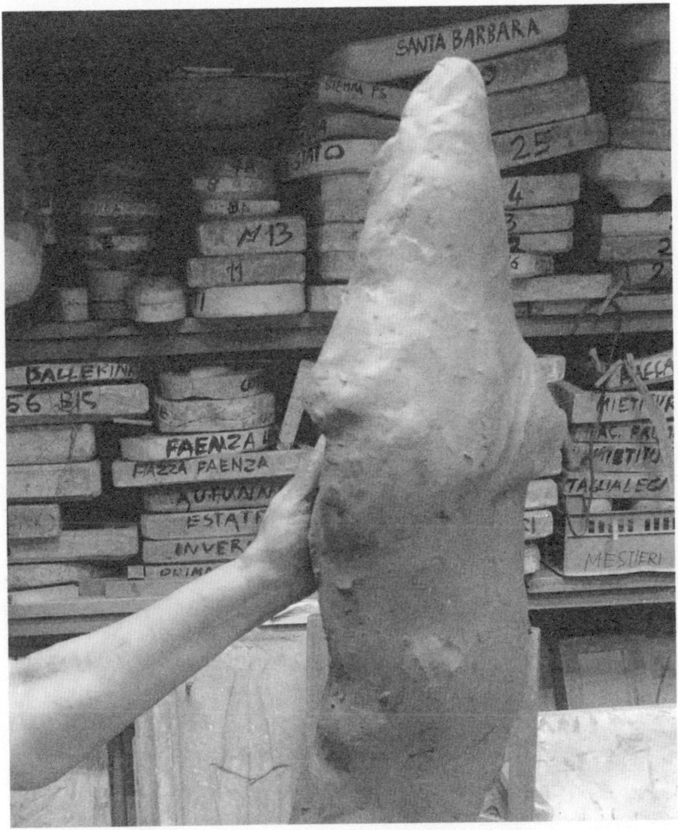

Simone Fattal, works in production, Ceramica Gatti, Faenza, February 2020

thinker like Martin Heidegger speaks of the world as the continuous apparition of being, these sculptures are what they are, but also "invented apparitions" that make us believe that they represent the marvel of life.

I should add that what is remarkable in the sculptures of Simone Fattal is their tenderness, the seemingly natural side of their forms. By "natural," one should not understand "curvy" or "gracious," but rather stable, necessary, adequate, not forced. I would also say distant. Sculpture is an art that can easily lean toward hardness, even brutality, except when it is made by real artists. Thus, for instance, one would not say of the big sculptures of Jean Dubuffet, like *L'Hourloupe*, that they are hard. They are light, because they come from the mind and address the mind. The same goes for Fattal's sculptures. They are created with integrity, following an internal law.

The sculptures of Simone Fattal are not in competition with those of other artists. They are

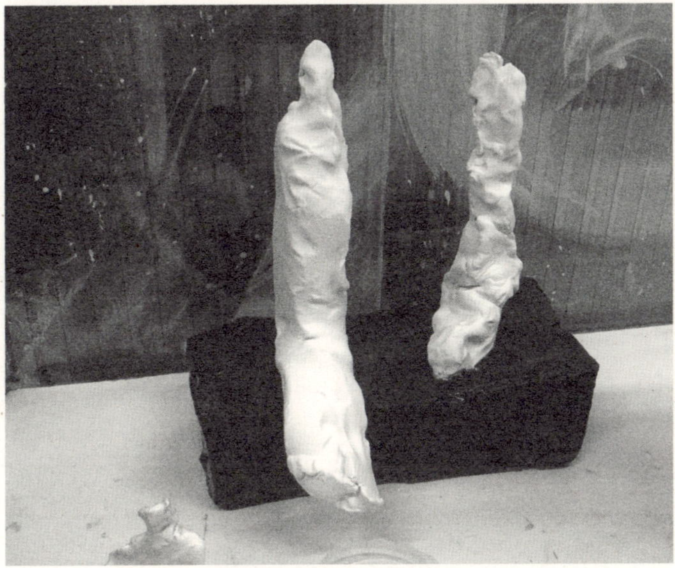

Simone Fattal, works in production, Ceramica Gatti, Faenza, February 2020

made in isolation and silence, in this state where the page is always white for the poet, in this state where one comes to the work having forgotten everything. It is as if while they were being made, nothing else existed besides the irrepressible need to create these forms, trusting that they will be naturally "inhabited." This process unknowingly gives a feeling that we are in front of archetypes.

Fattal also makes animals, lions that are shut off in another world, their own world, yet ready to leap. Heads of cows that suggest the animal in its entirety. She digs out of the clay the possibilities of life. She gives to voiceless earth a voice, a personality, and a soul. The secret of this impact comes from a knowledge that can only be instinctive, primordial. She does not fall into details, into what we call realism, and yet her characters are individualized and complete. It is a knowledge linked to instinct, generally lost if one gives precedence to technique to the detriment of spontaneity.

It is a knowledge that cuts through all we have learned to join the life which has informed the world. This possibility to join the world belongs to an ancient memory that most of us have totally lost. It is about finding a memory that numerous centuries have completely buried. To resuscitate this memory in privileged forms is a task that very few artists today have faced. Fattal's is an archaic world. And it is the one that true creators like Paul Klee or Constantin Brancusi have looked for, sometimes desperately.

Her world, archaic in appearance, is eminently contemporary. One can remember what Friedrich Nietzsche already said, that the one who belongs completely to their time, the real contemporary, is the one who does not coincide perfectly with it, but defines themselves as un-actual. This thought has been reworded

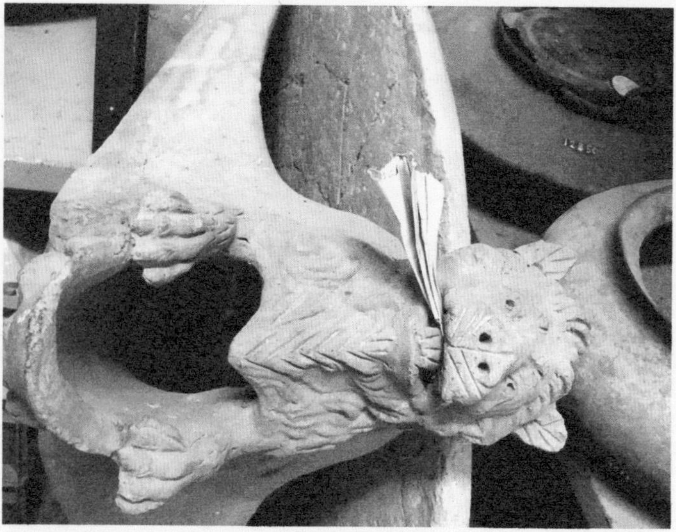

Simone Fattal, trip to Naples and Pompeii, February 2020

more recently by Giorgio Agamben, who said, "The contemporary is inscribed intact in the present, signaling it foremost as *archaic*, and only the one who perceives in the most modern and more recent things the traces or signals of archaism can be called contemporary."

We should also say that Simone Fattal's figures are of medium height. They can be held in one's arms. Recently she was able to work with a master craftsman, Hans Spinner, who is certainly one of the best ceramicists in Europe. Spinner has worked with the masters of contemporary sculpture, among them Eduardo Chillida, Antoni Tapiès, Jim Dine, Anthony Caro, Pierre Alechinsky, Jan Voss, Sean Scully, and others. Her collaboration with Spinner allowed Fattal to create pieces that are large in size, characters who seem to come with their animals out of the mythology proper to our regions, from Mesopotamia, Syria, as well as from the ancient ages of our history. But they are, at the same time, of today. They find their place among works pregnant with meaning, the masterpieces of sculpture in contemporary art.

Simone Fattal

Pompeii, Today

It took centuries to start looking at Pompeii again.

But the word, the event, was forever present in the imaginations of people around the world. Although forgotten, when it was "rediscovered," everyone knew what it was about.
For the destruction of Pompeii left a scar on everyone's imagination.
Why?

Pompeii represents what the word "destiny" signifies.
Something happens that comes from nowhere and cannot be stopped.

An event that concerns all, and which no one can escape.

It took years to start unearthing the site. But each time something was unearthed, people were confronted with what it means to be facing an instant, in destiny.

Unlike all the other archaeological sites, we can say that Pompeii already offers a reconstruction of itself, for the place was destroyed not by time, but by a moment.

The place is frozen in that instant. And the destruction preserved it.

Another irony.

Protected by the lava and debris, it was not looted and *disappeared* during the centuries, and when it *reappeared*, it *reappeared* intact.

One by one the monuments emerged, as they were on that day.

54

Today, November 22, 2020, I read in this fleeting news on my telephone: two new corpses found in Pompeii . . .

In 79 CE, the whole city of Pompeii was struck with an explosion. We can today qualify it as a nuclear explosion, and it destroyed the city entirely in a matter of hours, or two to three days. They heard the rumble and the noise, the earth was stirring and moaning like never before. No one understood what was going on or what was to happen.

One eminent woman, important enough to send an emissary in the first hours of the uncertainty and fears that were arising regarding the incomprehensible but dangerous-enough-to-worry signs—sent an emissary to Pliny the Elder, who was the prefect of the fleet posted nearby in Casties—for him to come and rescue her. Although he started immediately, he did not make it, but died on the way, probably from a heart attack due to the fumes and other dangerous materials. Some think she escaped, as a grave with her name was found not too far from Pompeii.

Death took different forms.

Was it destroyed in one instant? No, but what we see is an instant.
A moment in time, a moment in history as we can never witness anywhere else. An instant frozen for eternity. An instant comprising everything.

The life of a city. Its houses, monuments, temples, everything is there, as it was, from the same day. As if it had been photographed that day.

People were caught doing their daily routine. Or trying to escape.
We can witness the fear, the despair. The surrendering.

We can also witness their civilization as a whole. This also is rare.

57

Generally, ruins can be read on many levels, but there are fragments of all periods mingled together, or on top of each other. We need to reconstruct—level by level, fragment by fragment—their origins, relationships, and influences, the sequence in time. In Pompeii, it's a fixed image.

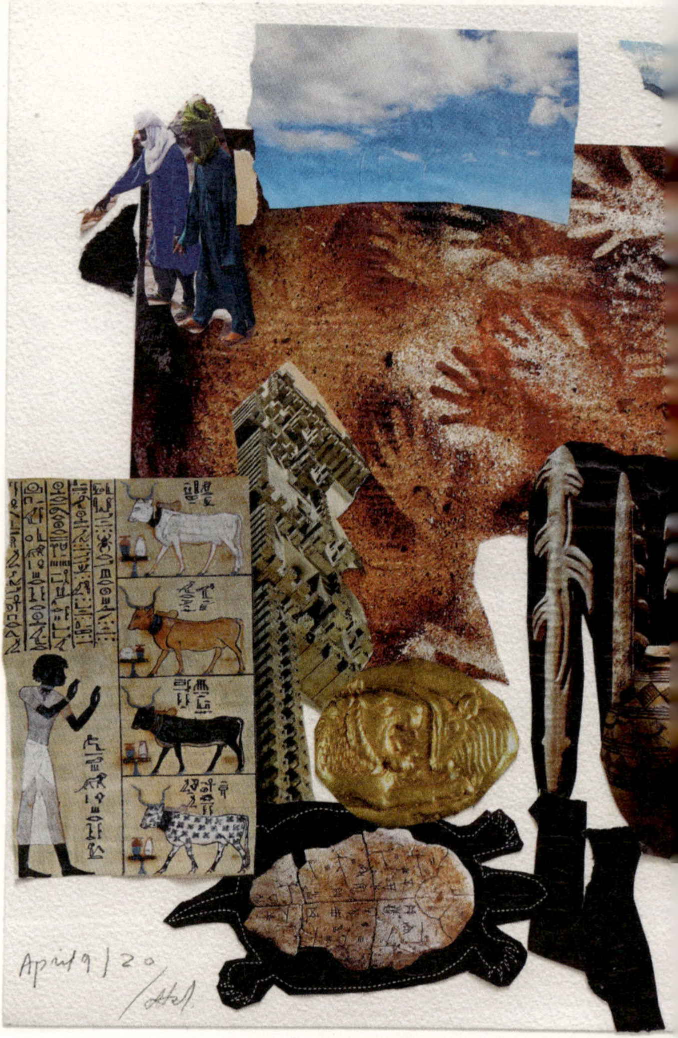
April 9 | 20

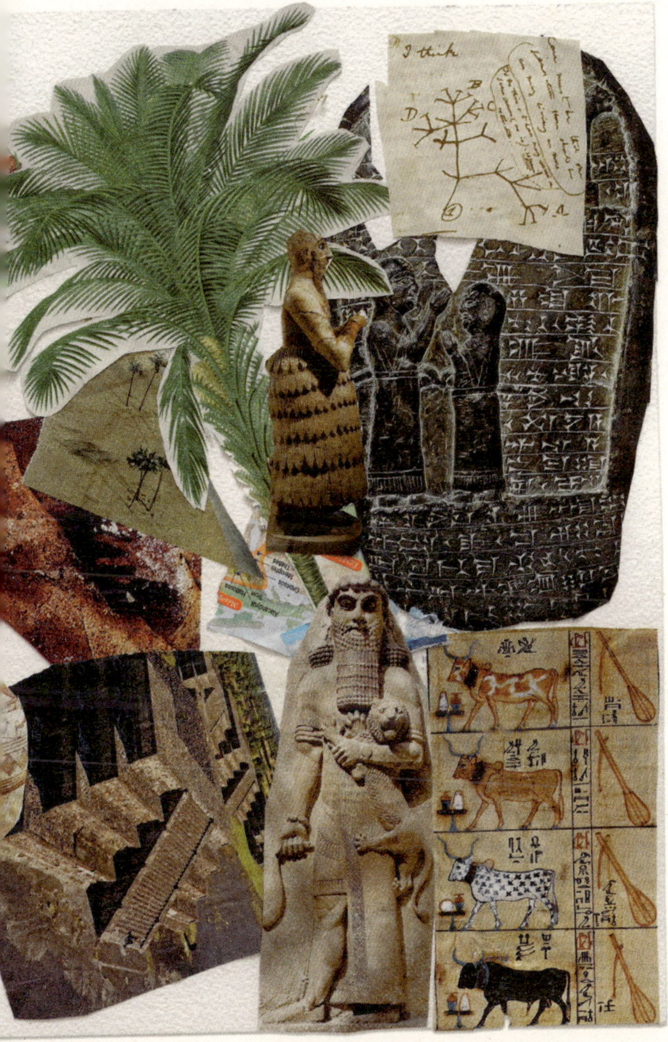
I think

I started discovering Pompeii by visiting the Naples archaeological museum.
The first thing that struck me was the paintings.
They, on the whole, express happiness.
These paintings, which to me prefigure the paintings of the Renaissance, reflect harmony, peace, and joie de vivre. Women, plants, flowers, music, myths.
Therefore, we can say that Pompeii society, rich and diverse, enjoyed a happy life. They were trading with all the harbors and cities of the Mediterranean.
By the sea and surrounded with fertile land, wine and olives and cereals and fruit were their produce and environment.

Their port was open to all trades and commerce, open to all civilizations, all the influences.
Different people from around the Mediterranean came to Pompeii, established commerce.
Sailors, merchants.

They also established temples, customs.
There was a pollination of all these different cultures.
Gods and goddesses from around the Mediterranean.
Their customs came and stayed, their artifacts also.

There was a political life, and we see and read electoral slogans.
A cosmopolitan city. A happy one.
We see an unusual number of houses that belonged to freed slaves. The theory is that a number of rich people had already left the city after the last earthquake, and that they had sold their houses to the freed slaves.
Carefree and modern.
We witness sexual freedom, political diversity, ethnic diversity.
And the importance of rich and wealthy women in their own right, who owned their houses

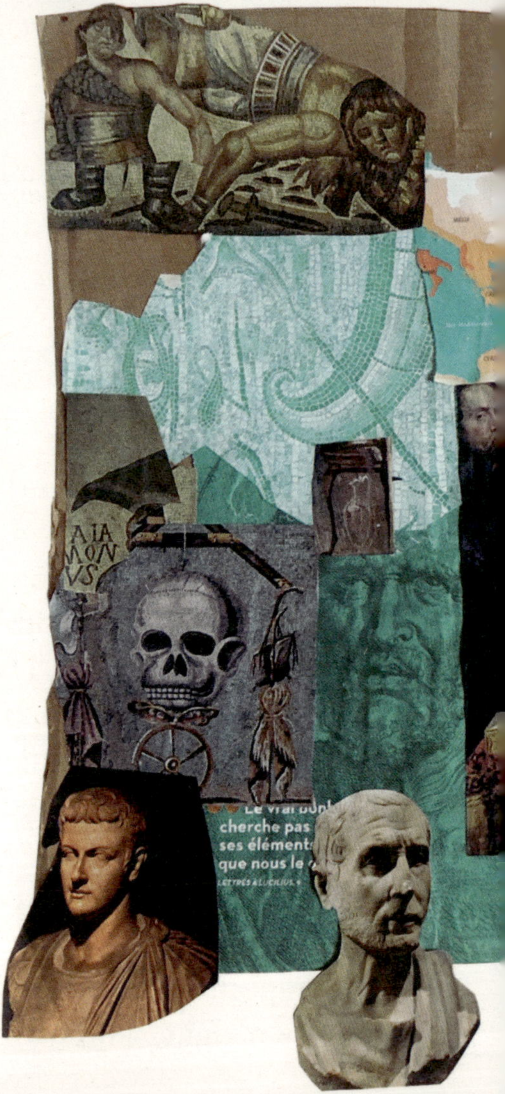
cherche pas
que nous le

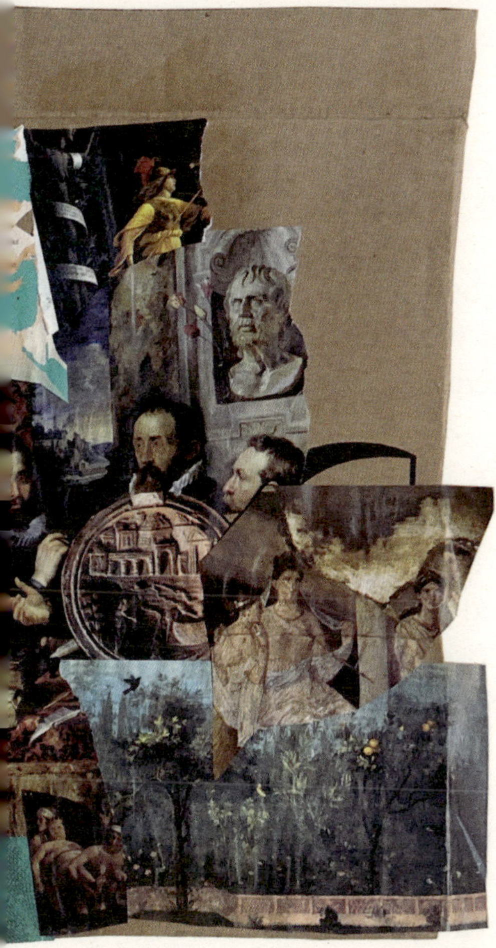

and businesses—as the example given above indicates.
Actually we witness the way of life.

Egypt is present, but also Syria, Lebanon, and Asia Minor. But with all this diversity and differences, it seems that all lived together in harmony.
It can certainly be a model for today.

Today all major European cities have also a fantastically varied population, but that seems to create major problems. On the contrary, it does not look as if Pompeii had a minorities problem.

The art was Pompeiian—that is, Roman, that is, Italian.
And as I said already, it will make its way to the Renaissance.

The temples are there, but also the houses.

And in them everything was left: utensils for cooking, pets, jewelry, beads, charms, art collections. These houses were for patricians. They belonged to rather rich people who collected sculptures and adorned their walls with paintings.

Life in its richness and variety was caught for us all to see and admire.
No other city in ancient history will give itself to the world so much, so well, and without artifice.

Rich and varied, opulent and bustling with life, Pompeii is also synonymous with death. This is the lesson we hear: death is with us and cannot be fought.

We just have witnessed another similar nuclear explosion on August 4 of this year in Lebanon.

At 6 pm, death struck, and struck violently. The whole city was not erased, but a portion the size of Pompeii was blown away, as in Hiroshima. Buildings and streets evaporated. Deaths and wounded abounded.

It was not Mother Earth, growling from the depths of its entrails, but the evil hand of evil.

Two opposite events.

This brings me to my sculpture.
My sculpture tries to recapture the living element of the moment that brought death.
My sculpture wants these moments to live eternally, being close to the place and that day, and give them back to life.

But what would I do if I were committed to making an artwork or an exhibition in Pompeii?
I would start with identifying its place in the Mediterranean.
One should (everyone should) read Edward Gibbon's *The History of the Decline and Fall of the Roman Empire* (1776). I read it because I know that the Roman Empire is mainly Syria, Egypt, Asia Minor, North Africa. The Roman Empire went also westward all the way to Britain, but the intense pollination and lasting effect was in the Mediterranean.
It started with the Hellenization brought to the Orient by Alexander the Great and his

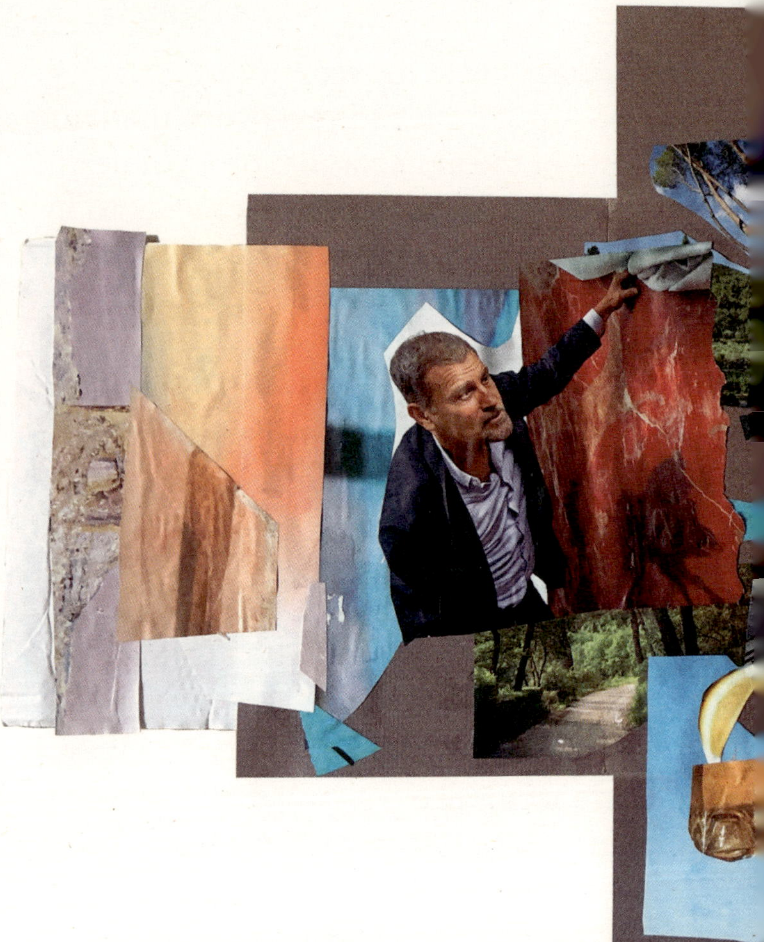

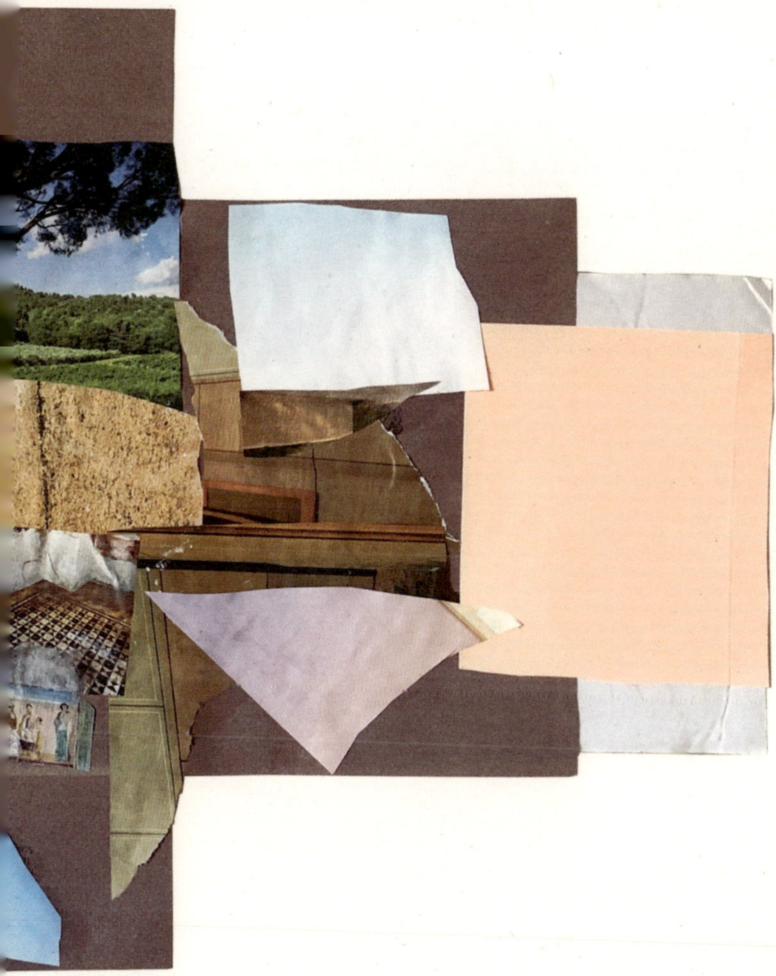

generals, and continued without any hiatus with the advent of Rome.
This is where the osmosis and the Roman civilization flourished and lasted the longest. This is where the largest examples of Roman architecture, interpreted by the Orient, took place: Baalbek, Palmyra, Basra Iskisham, Carthage . . .

When I first arrived at the Naples airport last February, a bit before the pandemic started, I noticed a magnificent replica of a Hermes sculpture.

He would be the first I am going to portray in my installation.

That day Hermes did not make it on time to warn the citizens of Pompeii of the imminent danger.

Then I would portray Isis at the bed of her father, trying to get from him, as he is sick, all the secrets of his power.

She will succeed.

And last but not least, many persons depicted on the walls of the House of Mysteries.
Why the House of Mysteries? Because there you read on the walls the story of the initiation of women to the rites of passage from girlhood to womanhood.
To the mysteries and rites of death.
The life cycles.

To finish with a monumental figure of Anubis, as he is painted on the walls of that house.

Anubis the guardian of death.

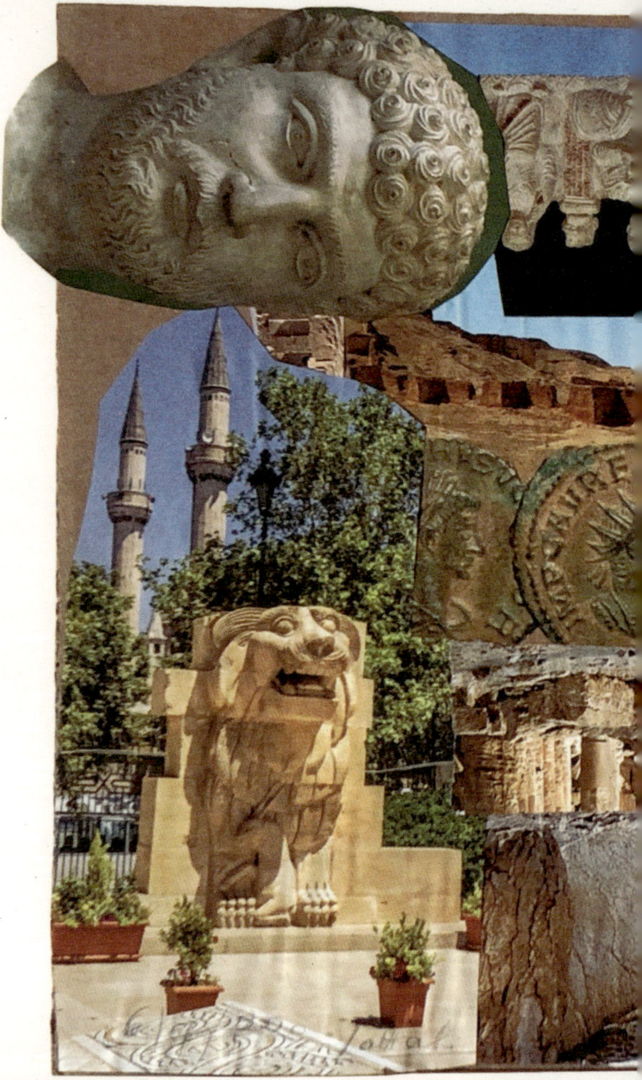

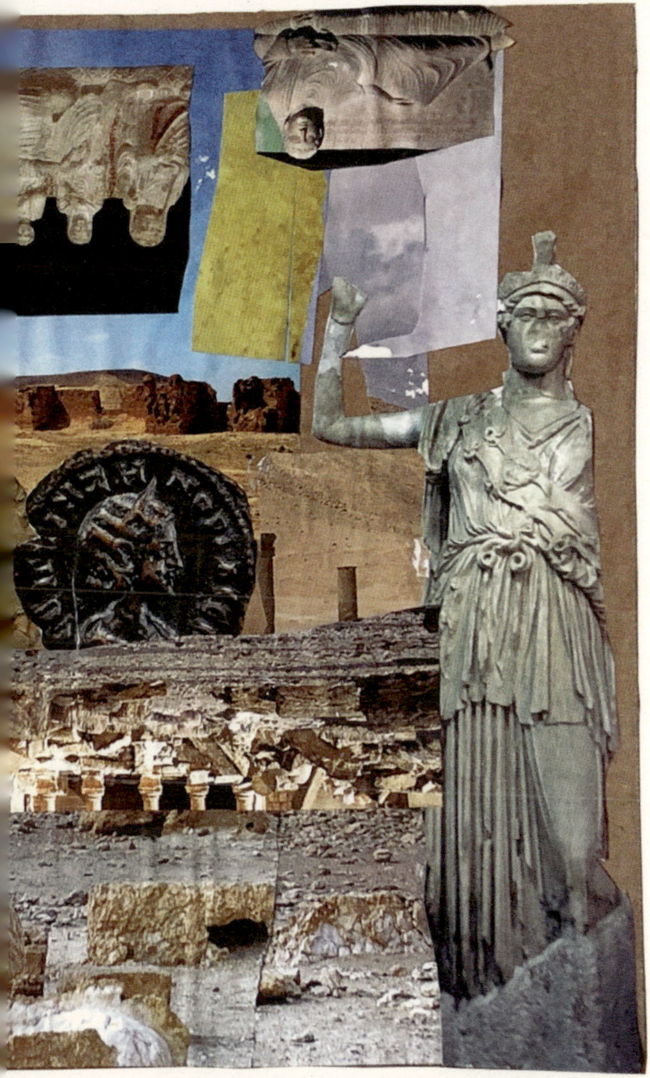

I would not finish on this note, but on a triumphant, beautiful (I hope) rendering of Apollo.

The god Apollo, god of music, love, and power.

Like Isis, he is portrayed with a lyre in his hand. One icon facing the other.

p. 58–59
Simone Fattal, *Under the Palm Tree*, 2020
Collage on found cardboard
p. 62–63
Simone Fattal, *The Roman World*, 2020
Collage on found cardboard
p. 68–69
Simone Fattal, *Hommage à Massimo Osanna*, 2020
Collage on found cardboard
p. 72–73
Simone Fattal, *A Walk Through the Ruins*, 2020
Collage on found cardboard
p. 76–77
Simone Fattal, *La Chouette Aveugle (The Blind Owl)*, 2020
Collage on found cardboard

All the images are Courtesy of the Artist and kaufmann repetto, Milan/New York

All the images were published on January 21, 2021 on the platform of the digital research center www.pompeiicommitment.org

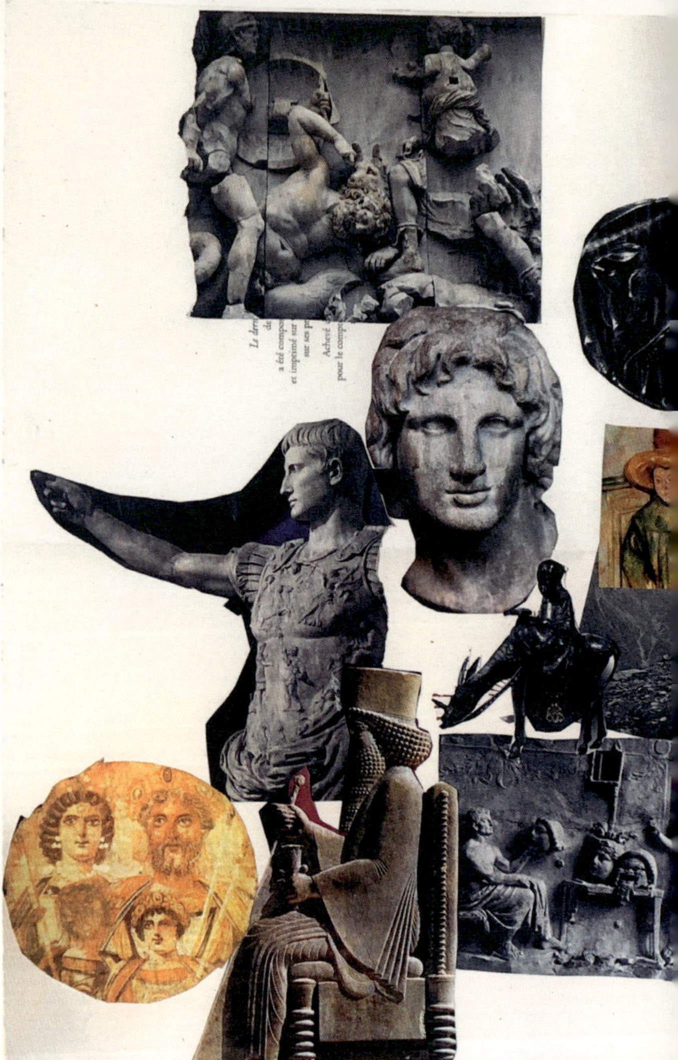

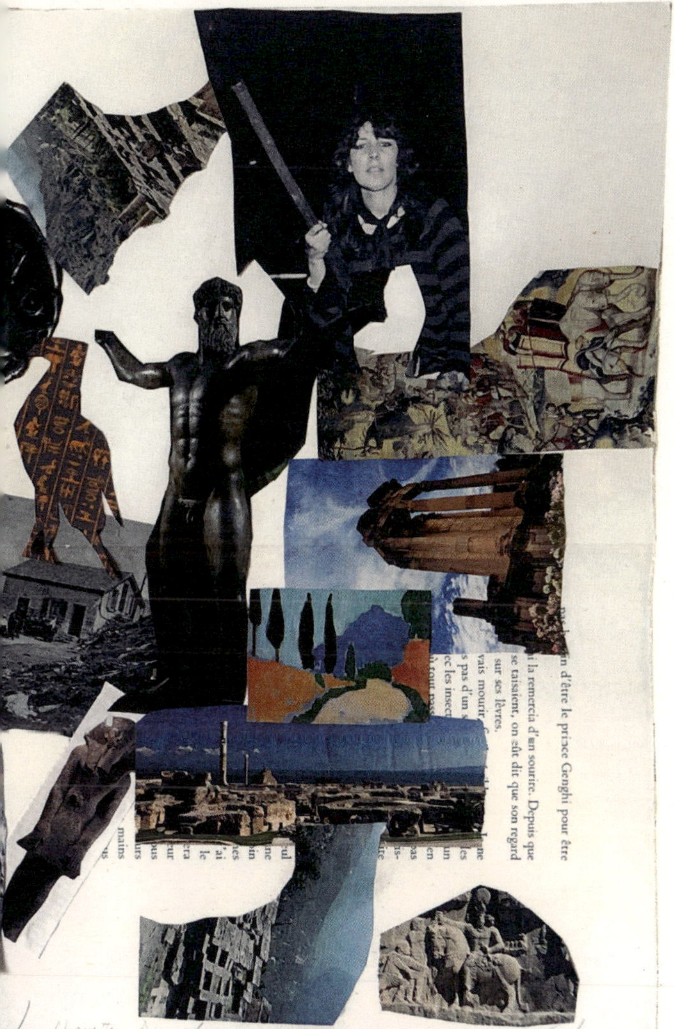

La Chouette Aveugle

Ep. 6 22/8/20

Fondazione ICA Milano

BOARD
Bruno Bolfo, Giancarlo Bonollo, Piero Gandini, Giovanna Maggioni, Giovanna Marianacci, Alberto Salvadori, Lorenzo Sassoli de Bianchi
PRESIDENT
Lorenzo Sassoli de Bianchi
VICE PRESIDENT
Bruno Bolfo
DIRECTOR
Alberto Salvadori
CURATOR AND EDITORIAL MANAGER
Chiara Nuzzi
PROJECT MANAGER & HEAD OF PRODUCTION
Clelia Colantonio
CURATORIAL AND PRODUCTION ASSISTANT
Gabriella Rebello Kolandra
ADMINISTRATION
BBS-Lombard stp srl
PRESS OFFICE AND COMMUNICATION
PCM Studio (partner Fondazione ICA Milano)
ARCHITECT
Luciano Giorgi LGB Architetti
DISPLAY
Gianluca Belloni, Emanuele Grillo

MAIN SPONSOR
INTESA SANPAOLO

SPONSOR
VALSOIA

DONORS
SANTA ROSA
FIN SALUTE S.R.L.
GRUPPO PROFILATI
GRUPPO IPAS

OFFICIAL APP
particle

PARTNER IN KIND
Facebook – Instagram,
Luisa Delle Piane

Fondazione ICA Milano counts on the collaboration of various professionals: the lawyer Ivan Frioni for the legal advice; Franco Broccardi for the tertiary sector.

POMPEII

Archaeological Park of Pompeii

GENERAL DIRECTOR
Gabriel Zuchtriegel
RUP
Silvia Martina Bertesago
DIRECTOR'S OFFICE
Ernesta Rizzo, Clelia Mazza
ADMINISTRATION OFFICER
Davide Russo
PRESS OFFICE, WEB & SOCIAL
Marella Brunetto
FUNDRAISING OFFICE
Maria Rispoli
PHOTOGRAPHY ARCHIVE
Giuseppe Scarpati
LIBRARY
Silvia Martina Bertesago
ARCHAEOLOGICAL STOREROOMS
Stefania Giudice
APPLIED RESEARCH LABORATORY
Valeria Amoretti
SCIENTIFIC AND ORGANIZATIONAL SUPPORT
Anna Civale
LEGAL SUPPORT
Domenico Costabile

ON THE COVER
Simone Fattal, *Villa of the Mysteries*, 2024, ink on paper. Courtesy of the Artist

POMPEIi COMMITMENT
Archaeological Matters

Pompeii Commitment. Archaeological Matters

CONCEPT
Massimo Osanna, Andrea Viliani
SCIENTIFIC CURATING
Andrea Viliani
EPISTEMOLOGICAL, CURATORIAL, EDITORIAL PROJECT AND MAINTENANCE
Stella Bottai, Laura Mariano, Caterina Avataneo
EDITORIAL COORDINATION
Art,em, CURA., Silvana Editoriale
PRESS OFFICE
PCM Studio
VISUAL IDENTITY, LOGO AND WEB DESIGN
amarantoweb.com

PARTNERS COMMITTEE
Nicoletta Fiorucci Foundation
Fondazione Sandretto Re Rebaudengo
(Team Partners)

THANKS TO
All the officers and collaborators, the front-of-house, fruition e surveillance staff of the Archaeological Park of Pompeii;
Giuseppe Barbella, Antonio Benforte, Tiziana Garofalo, Ilaria Improta (A. L. E. S.);
Marco Giglio (Università degli Studi di Napoli L'Orientale).

SPECIAL THANKS TO
kaufmann repetto, Milan/New York for their dedication and support of the exhibition and publication.

Simone Fattal. A breeze over the Mediterranean

PUBLISHED AND DISTRIBUTED BY
Mousse Publishing
Contrappunto s.r.l.
via Pier Candido Decembrio 28,
20137, Milan–Italy

AVAILABLE THROUGH
Mousse Publishing, Milan
moussemagazine.it

PUBLISHING EDITOR Ilaria Bombelli, Mousse
EDITORIAL COORDINATION Chiara Nuzzi, Fondazione ICA Milano
COPYEDITING AND PROOFREADING Emma Passarella, Mousse; Lindsey Westbrook
DESIGN Anna Azzali, Mousse
FIRST EDITION 2024
PRINTED IN ITALY BY Artigiana Grafica
ISBN 9788867493265
€ 25 / $ 30

ALL THE IMAGES
Simone Fattal, *A breeze over the Mediterranean*, installation view at Fondazione ICA Milano (September 8, 2021–January 9, 2022), a project by Fondazione ICA Milano in collaboration with *Pompeii Commitment. Archaeological Matters*
Courtesy of the Artist, Fondazione ICA Milano and kaufmann repetto, Milan/New York
Photo: Andrea Rossetti

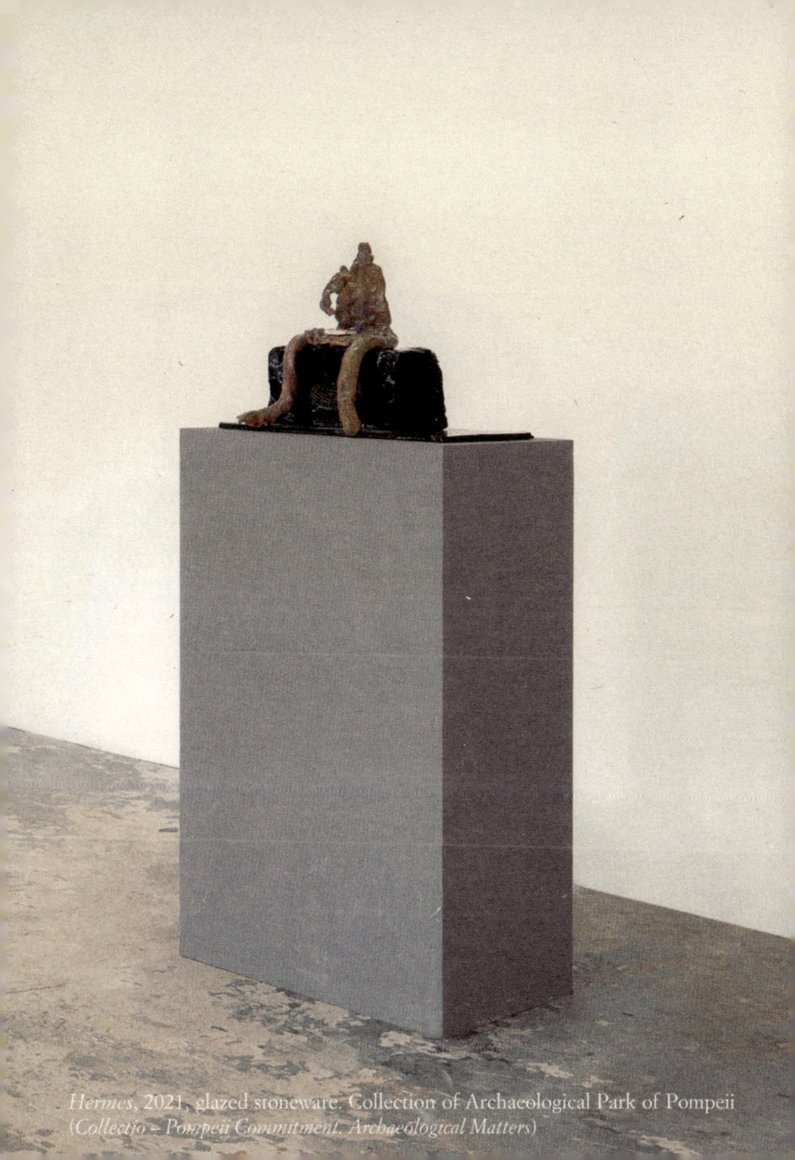

Hermes, 2021, glazed stoneware. Collection of Archaeological Park of Pompeii
(*Collectio – Pompeii Commitment. Archaeological Matters*)

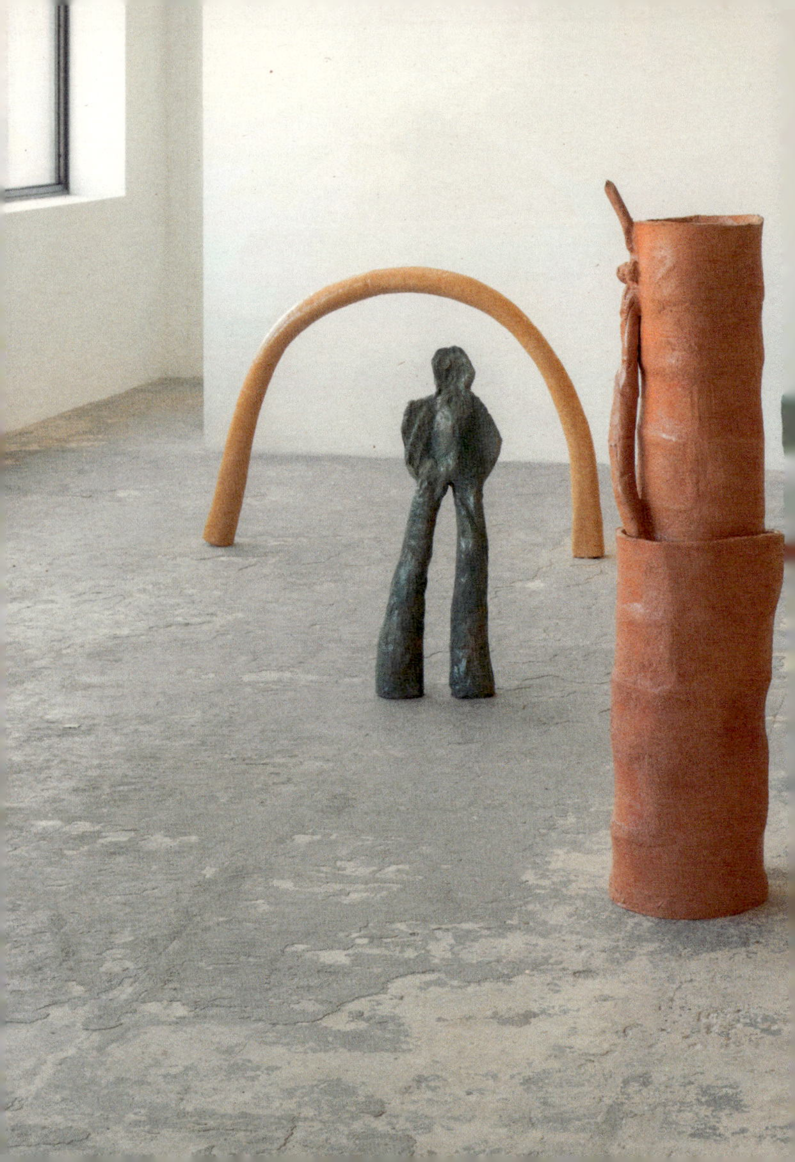

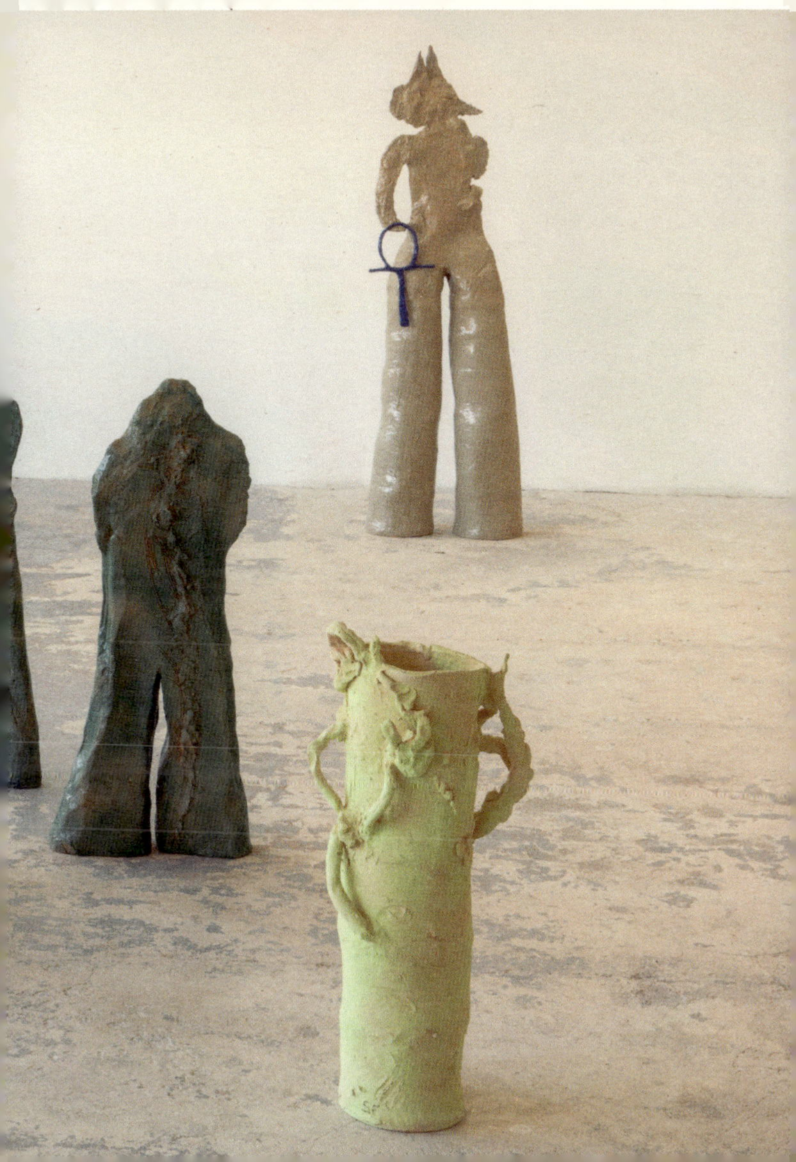

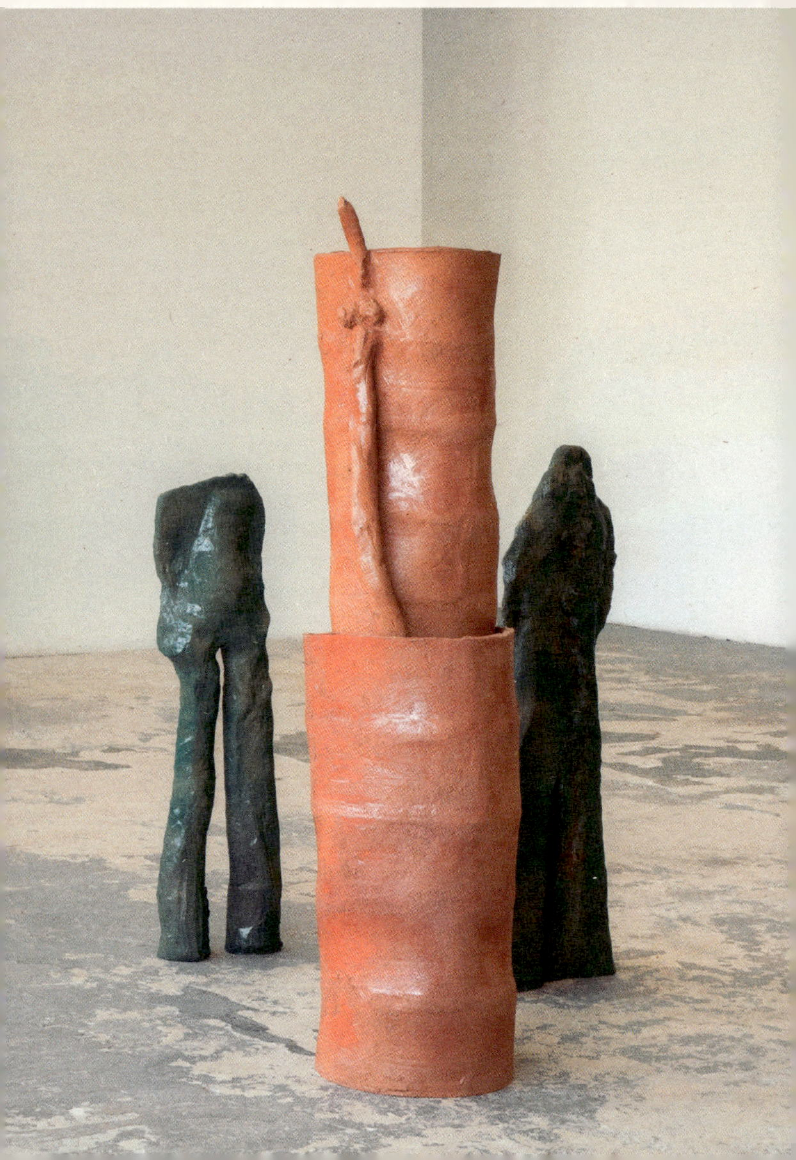

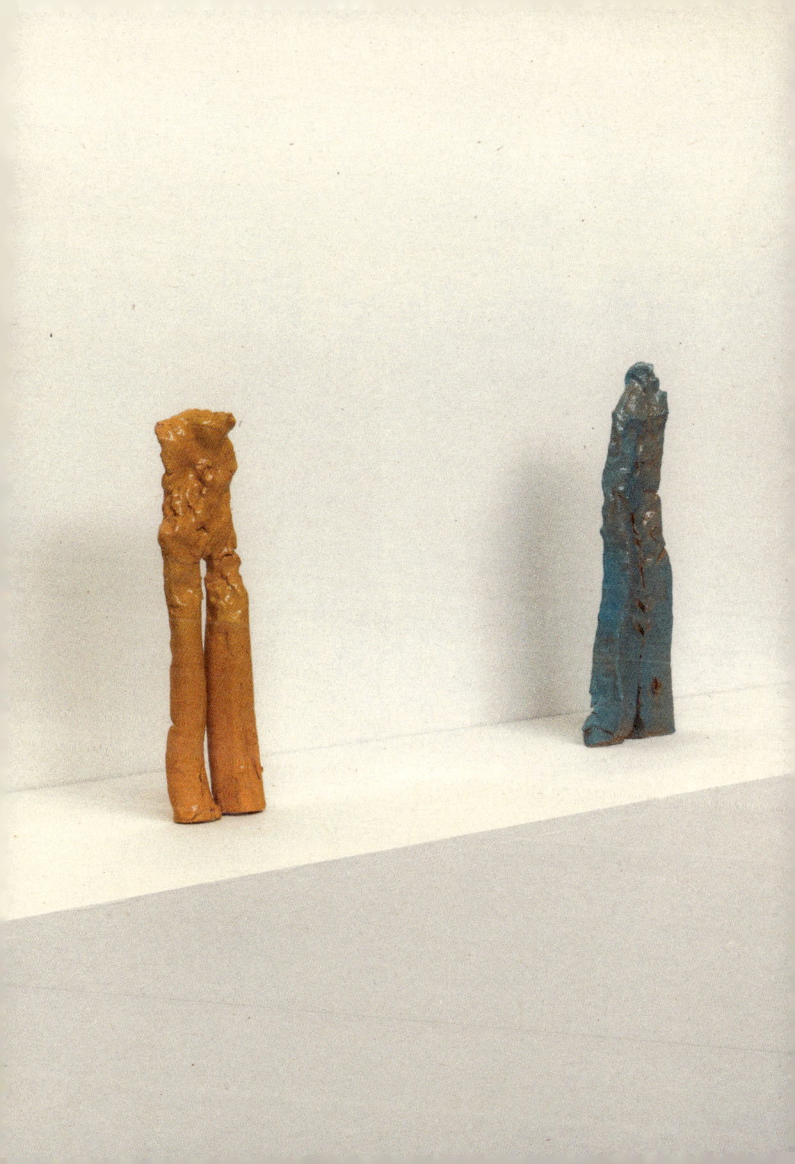

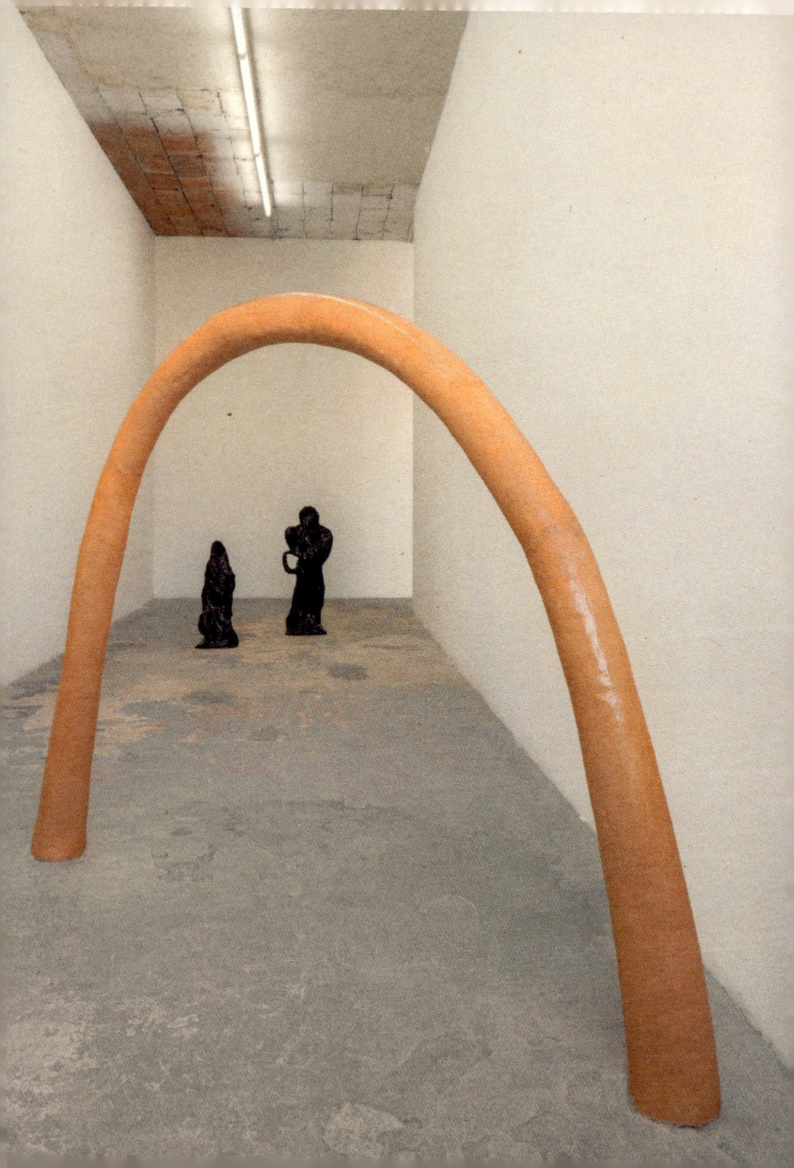

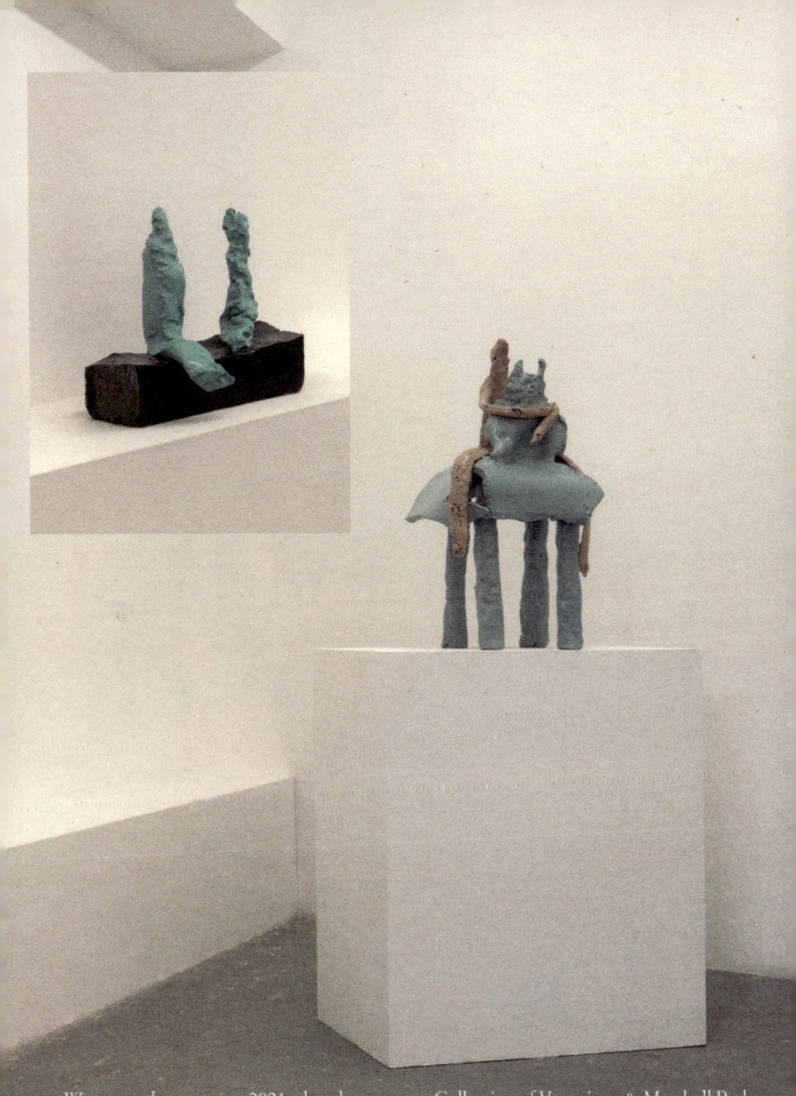

Woman and companion, 2021, glazed stoneware. Collection of Veronique & Marshall Parke
Europa and the Sacred Bull, 2021, glazed stoneware. Private Collection

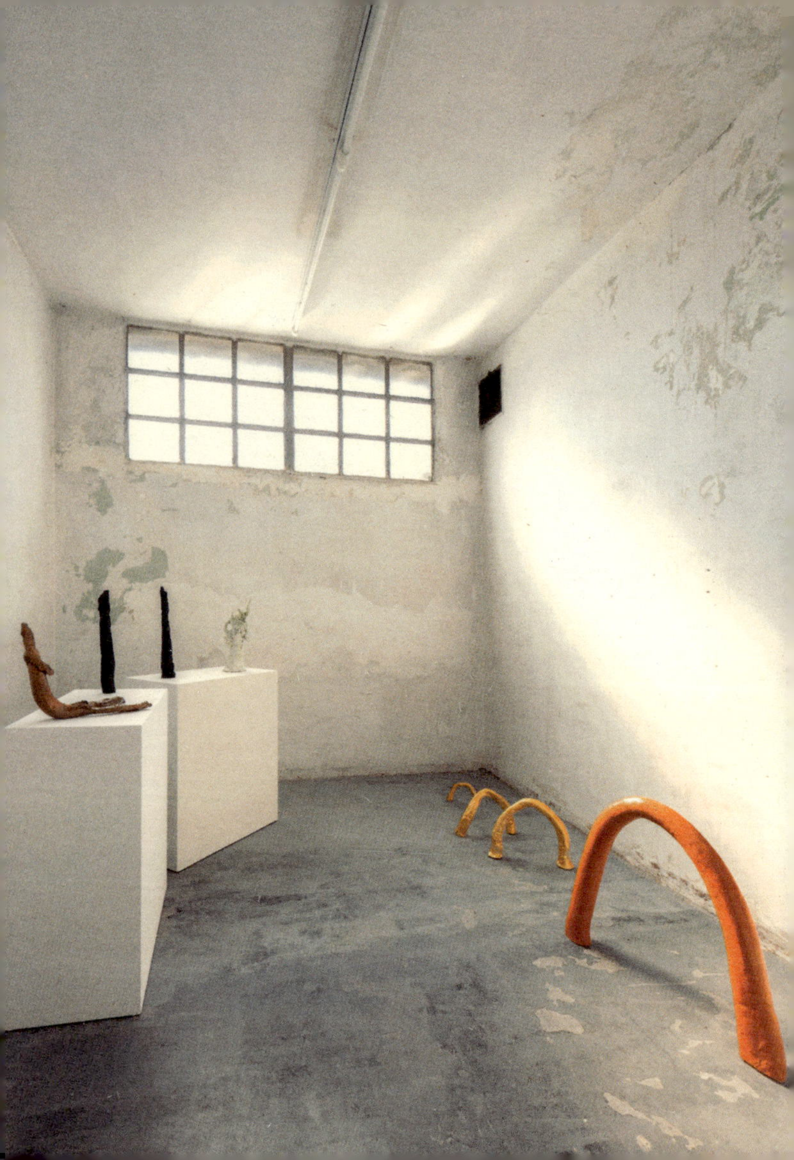

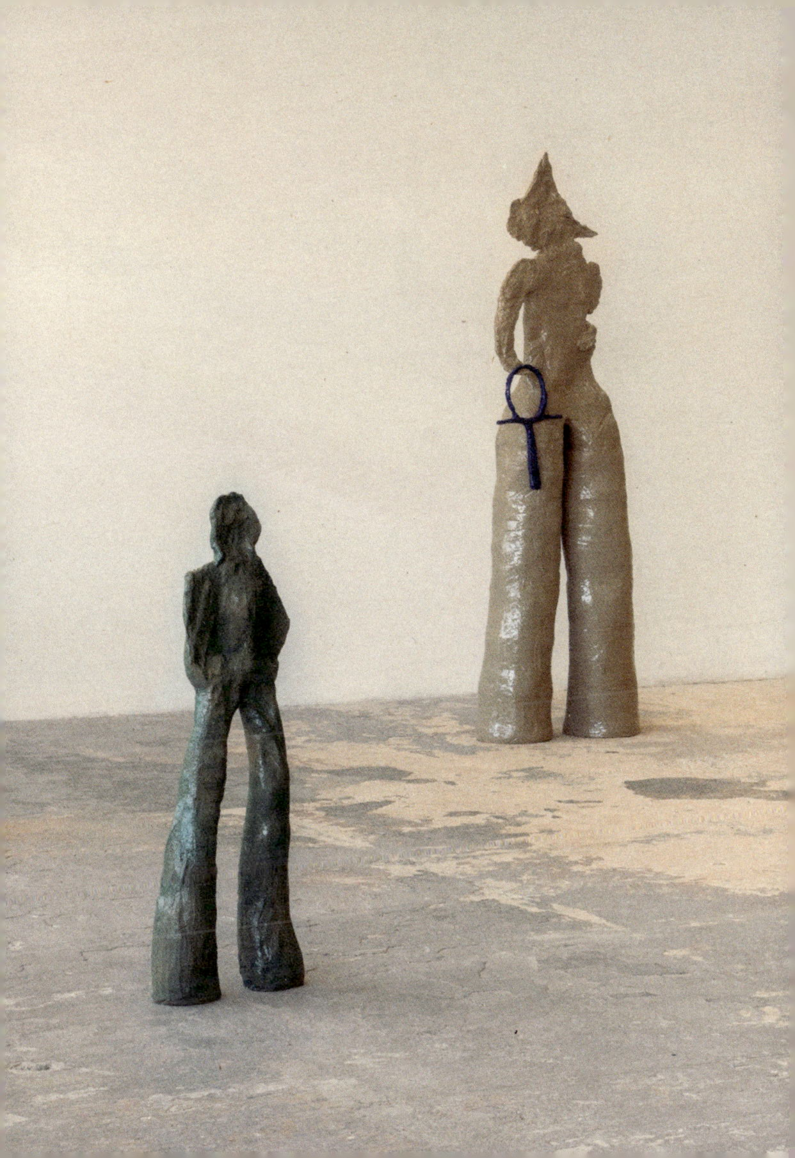

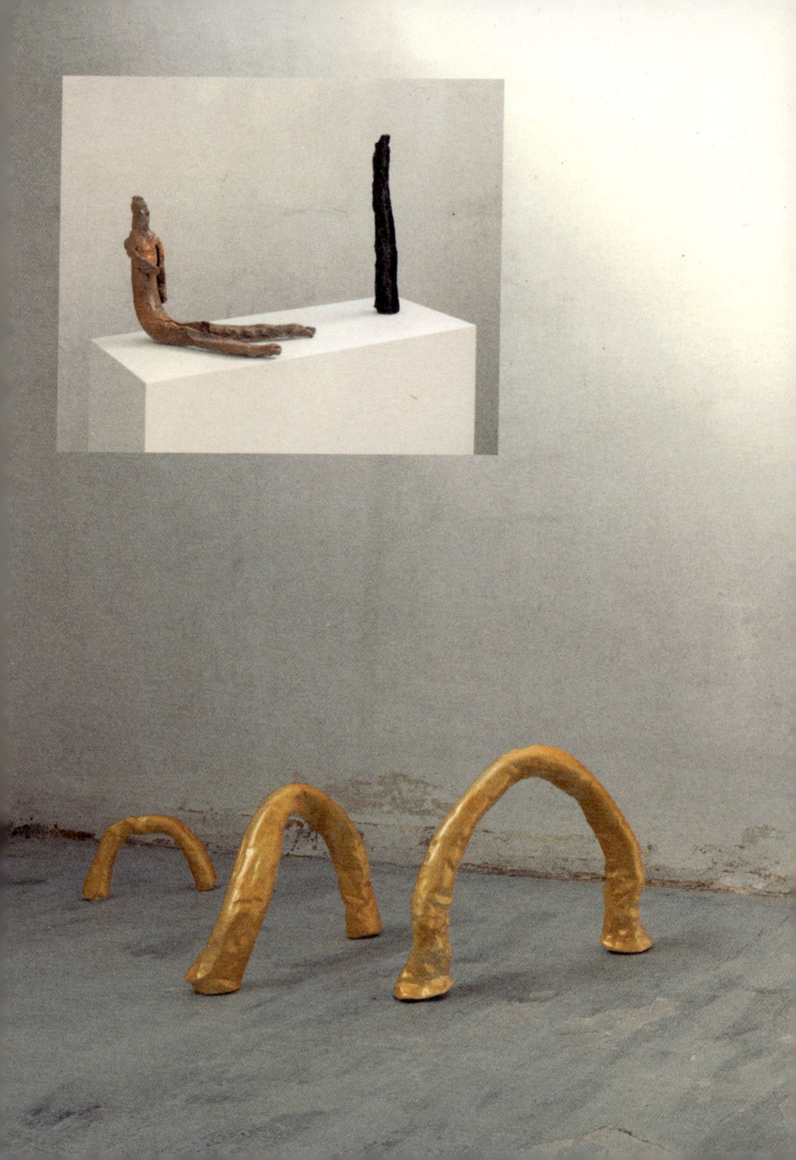

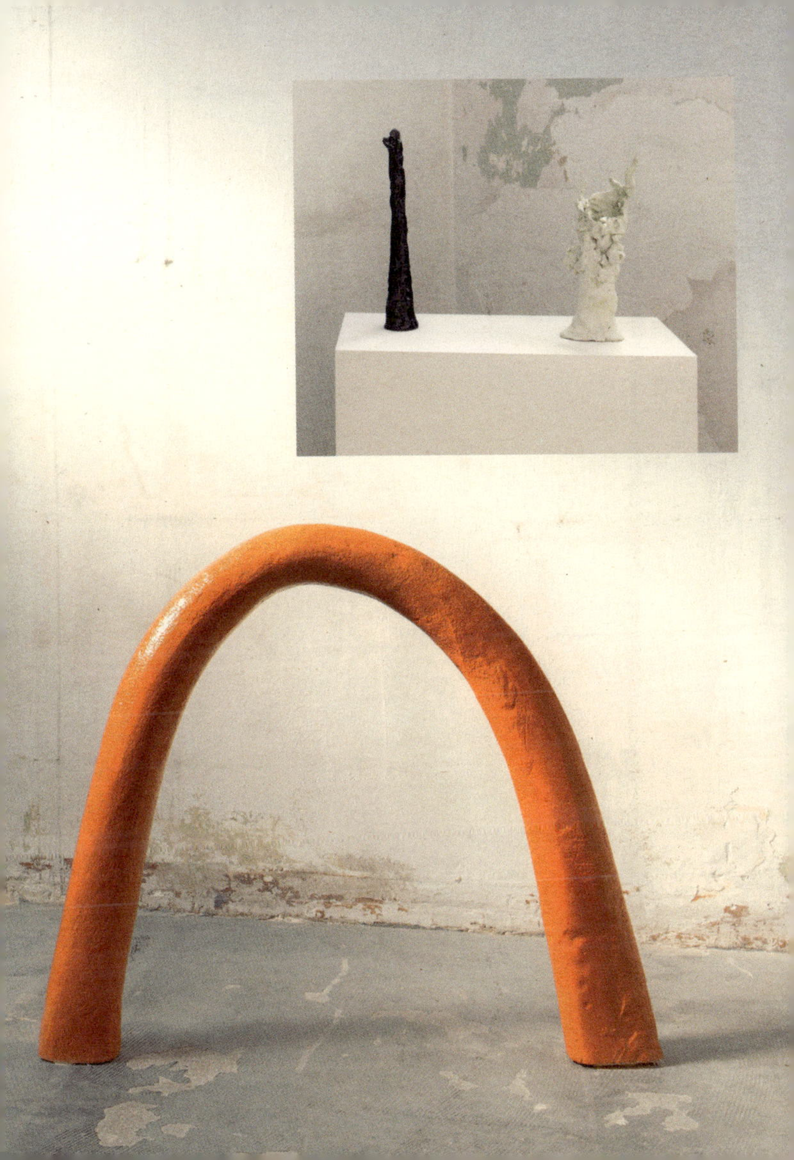

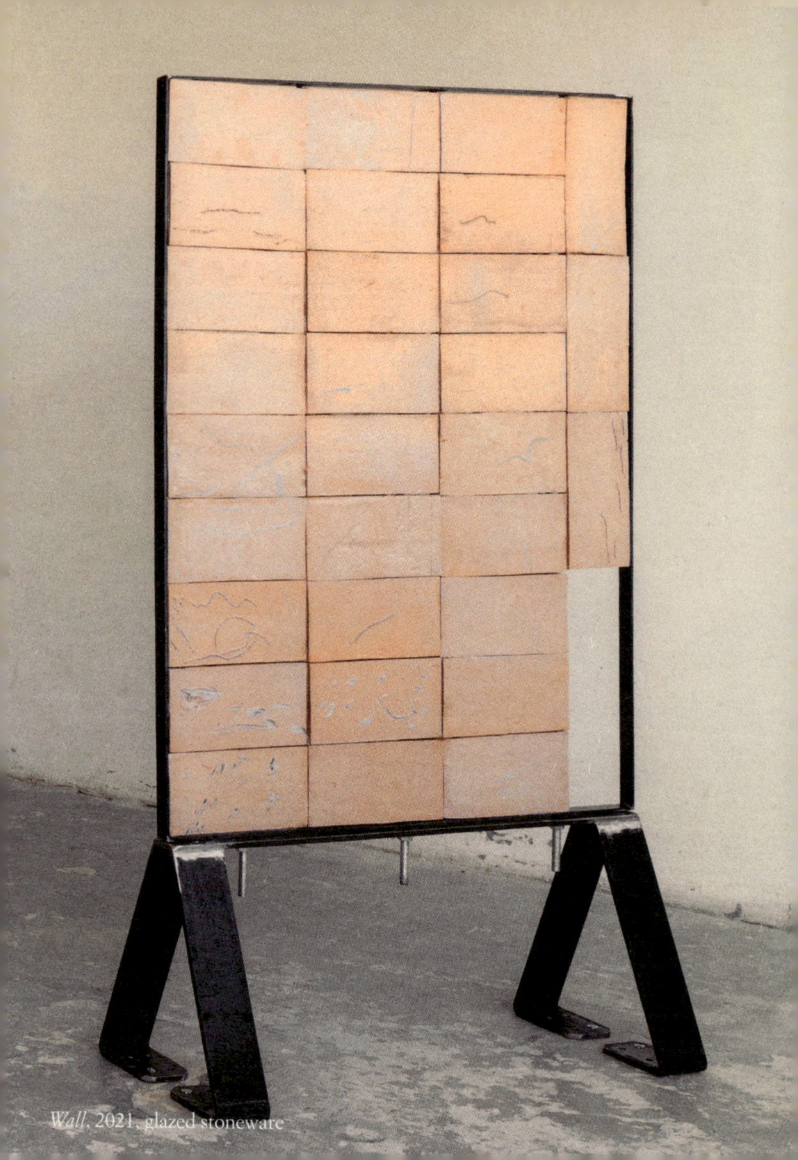

Wall, 2021, glazed stoneware

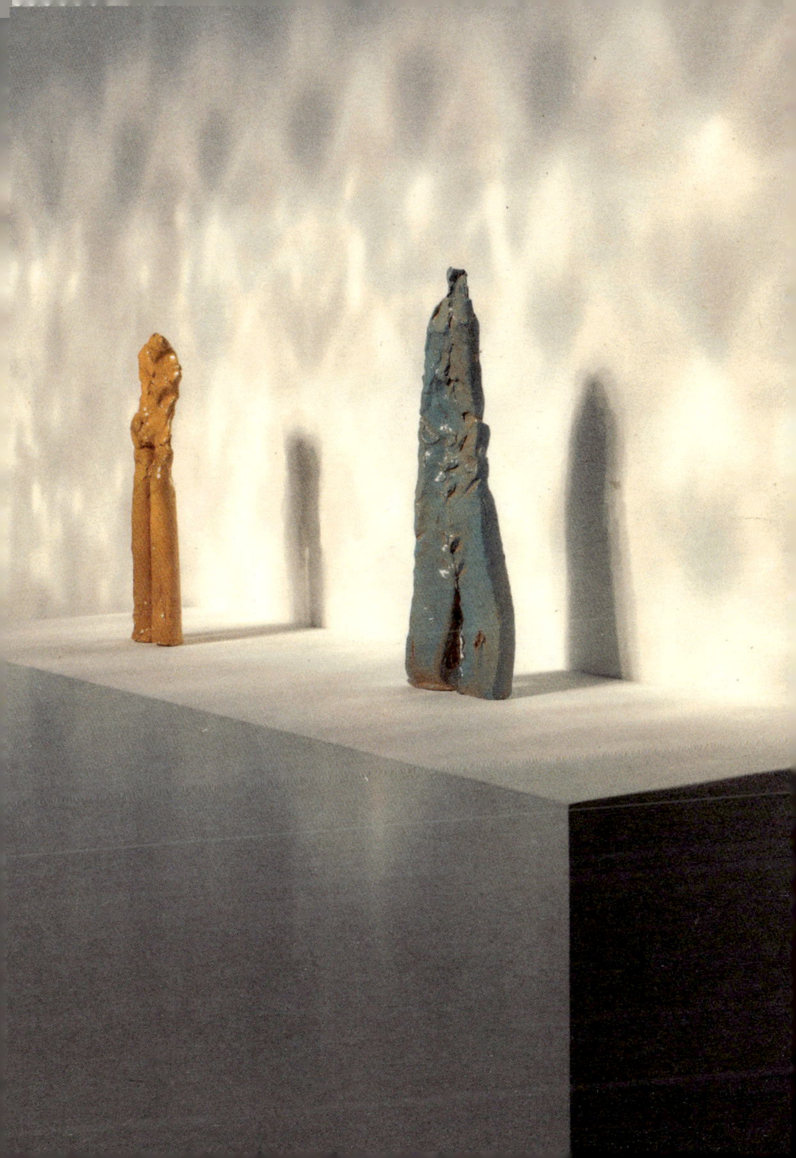

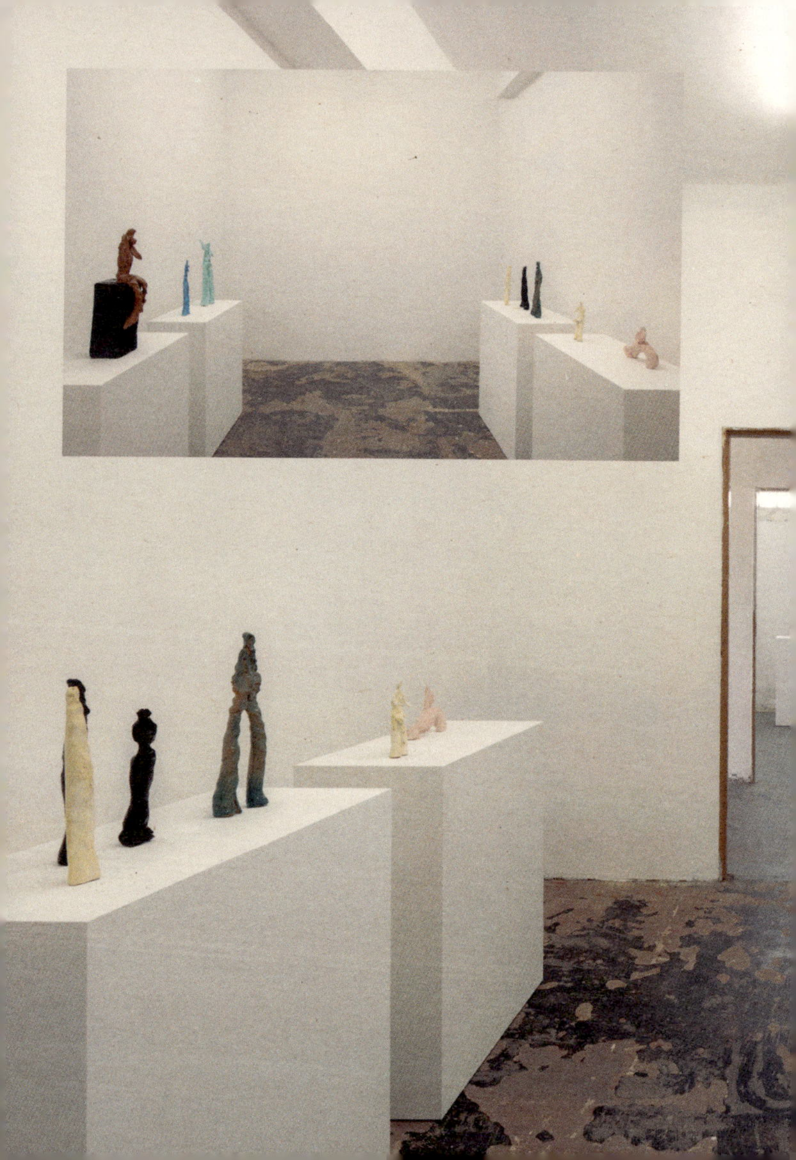